little explorers

Garden Wonders

A Guidebook for Little Green Thumbs

words & art by

Sarah Grindler

NIMBUS
PUBLISHING LTD.
— NIMBUS.CA —

Nimbus Publishing Limited
3660 Strawberry Hill Street, Halifax, NS, B3K 5A9
(902) 455-4286 nimbus.ca

Printed and bound in Canada

NB1618

Design: Jenn Embree
Editors: Emily MacKinnon and Claire Bennet

Library and Archives Canada Cataloguing in Publication
Title: Garden wonders : a guidebook for little green thumbs / words & art by Sarah Grindler.
Names: Grindler, Sarah, author, illustrator.
Description: Series statement: Little explorers
Identifiers: Canadiana (print) 20220453909 | Canadiana (ebook) 20220453918
ISBN 9781774711439 (hardcover) | ISBN 9781774711446 (EPUB)
Subjects: LCSH: Gardening—Juvenile literature.
Classification: LCC SB457 .G75 2023 | DDC j635—dc23

Nimbus Publishing acknowledges the financial support for its publishing activities from the Government of Canada, the Canada Council for the Arts, and from the Province of Nova Scotia. We are pleased to work in partnership with the Province of Nova Scotia to develop and promote our creative industries for the benefit of all Nova Scotians.

To Mum, Dad, Cathie, and Brad

Gardens can grow in so many places and in so many forms. Whether you have an apartment balcony or a big backyard, you can enjoy the delights a garden brings.

Let's go through the gate and explore how a garden grows and what you can create there.

Most gardens begin with soil, the loose layer of dirt where plants grow. In the soil there are decayed bits of plants and animals, broken bits of rocks and minerals, and billions of living organisms.

Some of these organisms you can see, while others like nematodes and protozoans are so tiny you need a microscope to spot them. Some that you can see include fungi, roots, and slimy, wriggly earthworms!

Nematode

A good sign that you have healthy soil is lots of slimy earthworms. With all their squirming about, they allow oxygen and moisture to get deep down where plants can spread their roots.

This nematode and protozoan eat bacteria and release nutrients to keep the soil healthy.

Protozoan

If your soil looks dry or crumbly, there are ways to give it more nutrients and minerals. Compost, wood ashes and wood chips, leaves, bone meal, and seaweed are all great fertilizers. Fertilizer is like a multivitamin for plants and it helps add good bacteria to the soil.

And who can forget poop! It sounds gross, but old livestock poop (also known as manure) is full of important nutrients from the food the farm animals ate. If you live in the city, you can buy bags of happy soil (worms not included) and bags of fertilizer from a garden centre.

Once you have healthy soil, it's time to plant some seeds and wait for them to germinate (sprout) into a seedling. These tiny seeds will grow into carrots; these ones, cucumbers; and these seeds will grow into ten-foot sunflowers! In order to germinate, seeds need sunshine and water.

Your seed packets will usually tell you how deep in the soil to plant your seeds, how far apart to space them, and what time of year is best to plant.

CARROT
Jack's Seeds
Bunnies Banquet

Cucumber
Annie's Seeds
Ladybirds Lunch

SUN FLOWER
Jason's Seeds
Bumble Bee's Breakfast

NASTURTIUM
Jack's Seeds
Hummingbirds Harvest

You will also need some tools to help you plant your garden, such as a watering can, pots, seeds, a cultivator to pull up weeds, a spade, and a pair of gloves.

Now you're ready to garden!

Let's plant this baby lavender plant.

First, dig a hole in the garden.

Next, water the empty hole.

Then pop in some fertilizer of your choice...

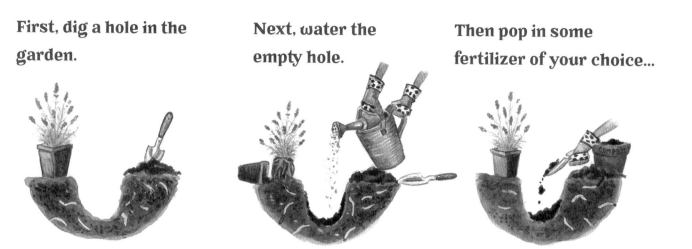

...and gently place your plant into the hole.

Cover up the bottom of the plant with soil and pat it down.

Then you can water the plant again.

Here are some helpful tips
for watering.

Plants are early risers, so give
them a drink in the morning at
the base of the stem so their
roots can soak it up.

If you wait to water until the heat of the day, the leaves can get sun damage, and if you water at night, the plants can get mildew.

If you are planting in a pot, you will need to make sure there are holes in the bottom so water can drain out, otherwise the plants can drown.

There are so many beautiful and delicious plants to grow in your garden. There are annuals (plants you plant every year, which last for a season or two, like sunflowers), perennials (plants that continue to bloom and grow every year, like hollyhock), and biennials (plants that take two years to bloom, like foxglove).

There are water plants (water lilies and irises),
shrubs and trees, spring bulbs (daffodils and tulips),
and succulents (like cacti).

Plants you can eat include root vegetables (carrots and parsnips), veggies that grow on vines (tomatoes and beans), leafy greens, fruits that grow on trees (apples), berry bushes, herbs and spices, and so many more!

But in order to grow your fruits and veggies, you will need help from a few lovely garden guests.

Bees, butterflies, hummingbirds, ladybugs, and many other insects are called pollinators, and they are all friends of the garden. Without them plants would not be able to grow. Pollination occurs when sweet nectar from the centre of the flower attracts hungry pollinators. They collect the powdery pollen from one blossom and distribute it when they visit the next plant, which helps the plants make more plants!

red slug

There are other creatures you can find in the garden that can be a little less helpful. Certain types of caterpillars, tiny aphids, bunnies, slugs, certain birds, wood bugs, deer, and many more also enjoy munching on your hard-earned produce.

plant squisher

rabbits

squash beetle

starlings

aphids

But there are some gentle ways to
stop these guests if you don't feel like
sharing your harvest.

cabbage
moth

cucumber beetle

red slug

potato beetle

deer

Luckily, lots of these methods involve tasty snacks for those welcomed garden guests I mentioned before. Aphids, for example, are a favourite snack for ladybugs. And if you plant nasturtiums in your veggie bed, they will lure the aphids away from your other plants.

Some caterpillars may just need to be picked off plants by hand, or you can knock them off with a shower from the garden hose. Make a scarecrow, cover your crops with nets, or build a fence so bigger and hungrier guests, like bunnies and deer, stay out. Another great way to dissuade these critters is something called companion planting.

Companion planting isn't just useful for attracting and dissuading critters. Plants can enjoy friendships too! Indigenous Peoples have known about companion planting for centuries. They know to plant "The Three Sisters" (corn, beans, and squash) together.

This is because the corn creates a sturdy stock for the beans to climb, the beans bring much-needed nitrogen to the soil, and the squash shades the soil and keeps away those pesky critters. Teamwork!

Here are some fun gardening projects
you can try!

❀ Plant strawberries in a hanging basket
or grow a tiny herb garden in a window box.

❀ Make a sweet pea teepee in your
backyard using bamboo and string.

There are lots of ways you can attract pollinators, even if you live in the city.

❀ Hang a hummingbird feeder and fill it with a mixture of 1 part sugar dissolved in 4 parts water.

❀ Set up a birdbath.

❀ Plant a butterfly garden in an old boot or watering can full of flowers that pollinators love, like cosmos and marigolds.

There are so many types of amazing gardens.
Creative gardens are everywhere, and you don't
need a lot of space to plant your very own.

What would you like to grow?